CW00470135

Health Econo
Unini

Tony Lockett
Associate Director
Health Economics

RADCLIFFE MEDICAL PRESS
OXFORD and NEW YORK

Radcliffe Medical Press Ltd
18 Marcham Road, Abingdon, Oxon OX14 1AA, UK

Radcliffe Medical Press, Inc.
141 Fifth Avenue, New York, NY 10010, USA·

Reprinted 1996

British Library Cataloguing in Publication Data

A catalogue record for this book is available from the British Library.

ISBN 1 85775 069 1

Library of Congress Cataloging-in-Publication Data

Lockett, Tony.
    Health economics for the uninitiated / Tony Lockett.
      p. cm.
    Includes bibliographical references and index.
    ISBN 1–85775–069–1
    1. Medical economics.   I. Title.
    RA410.L63   1996
    338.4′33621 - - dc20

95–52776
CIP

Typeset by Marksbury Multimedia Ltd, Midsomer Norton, Bath, Avon
Printed and bound by Biddles Ltd, Guildford and King's Lynn

Contents

Preface

Health and health care are two of the dominant political and economic issues in many countries at the present time. Most nations have faced a rapid rise in health care expenditure over the past 30 years, and it is not surprising that health economics as a specialty has shown a rapid expansion. Health economics has been defined as how resources are allocated to health-related issues, and there is now a considerable amount of time, effort and energy devoted to it. Most professionals in the health care industry are exposed to its various analyses and statements in the form of articles, promotional material and governmental guidelines. Despite this, there is a poor understanding of what health economics can and cannot do. The purpose of this book is not, therefore, to train health economists but to provide a practical guide to the understanding of health economic issues and to the examination of articles and other literature without terror.

This book has evolved from lectures that I have given throughout the South and West RHA that have aimed to provide a wide range of discussion to a diverse a group as DHA executives and non-executives, doctors and NHS managers. The book therefore has no particular group of health care professionals in mind but aims to serve as a general introduction for all levels. For those who wish to take it further, there is suggested further reading at the end of each chapter.

The book has the general structure of first providing a discussion about general economic principles, second discussing the applications of these principles to the area of health care, and finally using these principles in health.

I would value any comments, signed or otherwise, and also guidance on anything thought to be omitted. Undoubtedly, I have simplified many of the issues – in order to keep the theoretical content of this opus to a minimum and to open the world of health economics to all readers.

Tony Lockett
Southampton
January 1996

1 An introduction to economic thinking

> **Key points**
>
> *The reform of health care has led to increased interest in health economics. Health economics as a discipline requires some definition that closely relates the problems in hand. This chapter provides a basic understanding of health economic concepts.*

What is economics anyway?

Economics is a very broad subject, covering everything from the behaviour of governments to the choices made by people shopping in their local supermarket. Therefore, to attempt to define economics in one globally meaningful paragraph is perhaps a little ambitious. In an attempt to simplify the situation, economics can be subdivided into two main disciplines. Macroeconomics is concerned with the behaviour of large aggregates, such as countries, and the behaviour of large groups within them, for example the European labour market. This contrasts with microeconomics, which looks at the behaviour of parts of the 'big' picture; it is concerned with the behaviour of individuals and organizations. The position of health care within this classification is complex. Clearly health care is a big industry – governments are very concerned about the effect of health care expenditure on the gross national product. However, for the most part, health economics seeks to focus the choices made by individuals within the health system and thereby look at its total effect. This book will stay with this convention and mention the macroeconomics aspects of health care only in passing.

Why microeconomics?

Microeconomics is based on the construction of *models*. These models seek to 'explain the behaviour of economic actors, and the aggregation of their actions, in different economic frameworks'.

What are the elements of a health economic model?

The somewhat wordy definition above introduces the basic elements of a microeconomic model: actors, behaviour and frameworks (also called institutions). It also implies the achievement of an overall explanation of the aggregation of actions (often termed equilibrium). For a microeconomic analysis to be valid, these four elements must be present, and it is worthwhile exploring each element further.

Actors

These actors may be either individuals or firms (meaning businesses) who seek to exchange resources for goods or services.

Behaviour

For an analysis to be meaningful, the actors must be able to make choices. Furthermore, the actors must be able to make a choice that achieves some desirable end. This desirable end (or outcome) varies with the nature of the actor. In economic terms, an individual actor is said to have a *preference* for a good or service that gives satisfaction. In economics, satisfaction is often termed *utility*. The individual actor behaves in such a way that utility is maximized, given that there is usually only a finite amount of money available, termed a *budget constraint*. Microeconomics for the individual, therefore, could be said to be about choice under scarce resources.

The microeconomic analysis of firms as actors takes a different stance. Firms, which include companies, hospitals and institutions, act to maximize profit – or something that represents profit. Firms act under a different set of constraints, set by how they produce goods and services and the technological limitations of that process.

These models of the behaviour of individuals and businesses are often accused of being simplistic and insulting. Consumers do not walk down supermarket aisles measuring their utility and even the most hard-nosed boss is not driven solely by profit. However, despite the shortcomings of the models, they are still useful in looking at economic behaviour. First, the departure of economic actors from these ideals tells us something with reference to a fixed point, i.e. the model. This makes measurement considerably easier. Second, why individuals act is not important – providing they act within the models as if they were maximizing utility. Finally, experimental evidence has shown that deviations from the models are often slight, and when they are aggregated, these deviations often cancel out.

Institutions

The choice of an individual will depend on the range of opportunities that he or she is presented with, which will depend to some degree on the choice of others. This linkage is described in economics as the institutional framework. The institutional framework, in addition to describing the general nature of the options available, seeks to link those options to the outcome of others' actions.

Examples of institutional frameworks abound in economics, the most ubiquitous example being markets. Markets are institutions that permit exchange of goods and services. However, the choice available in a market is determined by what goods are brought to sell at the market, which is determined by the price commanded, which is linked to the amount sold. This degree of interdependency makes markets of all types ideal institutional frameworks, even where the market may not be working perfectly – as in health care.

Equilibrium

Having described the individuals, their choices and the outcomes of that choice on the wider population, equilibrium seeks to describe the result of the sum of the activities involved. The result is usually defined in terms of an *equilibrium analysis*. This term encompasses a range of techniques that is the subject of later chapters. Generally speaking, however, the analysis seeks to determine the point at which an actor is doing the best he can, given the behaviour of all other actors around. This point is normally described in terms of the utility achieved or profit made. It is important to stress that, in all forms of economic analysis, there is no assumption that this equilibrium is actually achieved. Instead, the emphasis is on stressing where the role of equilibrium in determining actions may be important.

The purpose of microeconomic analysis

Having described the basics of microeconomics, what do we do with microeconomics: what will be the outcome of all this theory? The simple answer is to say that it increases understanding. This understanding has two aspects. First, it can lead to better business practice. Some executives use microeconomic techniques to gain better understanding of the markets that they are in and look for ways to improve business outcomes. Second, the study of microeconomics is a valuable social tool to assist in the determination of policy for better social outcomes.

The dimensions of this understanding in economics, as in any other science, are the *explanation* and *prediction* of observed phenomena. Therefore economic analysis may be either *positive* or *normative*.

What questions fit what models?

Questions regarding the choices made by actors under various economic situations, and the logic and motives underlying those choices, are examples of positive analysis. Positive analysis also deals with the prediction of the behaviour of consumers, for example the effects of tax rises on the numbers of car purchases. Positive analysis is either right or wrong; the results of positive analysis can always be checked against the data available. However, real world data are often ambiguous, and it is often difficult to tell whether a prediction has actually been fulfilled.

Positive analysis is not, however, the whole story, and we often wish to go beyond the description of a situation and pass judgement upon it. When doing this, we are seeking to say whether a situation is desirable or undesirable. We may also want to compare alternative situations and say something about the relative merits of the alternative choices. Finally and most importantly, we may wish to design policies that minimize or eliminate the waste of resources. Normative economic analysis seeks to enable these questions to be answered. Normative analysis is vital to situations where markets fail to ensure that resources are justly distributed in the eyes of society, i.e. where competitive mechanisms lead to an unjust distribution of resources and policies or laws are required to ensure that resources and outputs are distributed in such a way to achieve socially desirable ends.

The scope, detail, emphasis and complexity of microeconomics

The sky knows no limits as far as microeconomic analysis is concerned, but before an analysis is embarked upon, it is important to consider the role of the scope, detail, emphasis and complexity of any analysis. The characteristics determine how an economist looks at the world and also define the limitations to any analysis.

It is perfectly possible to construct an analysis involving the interchange of five goods; say apples, pears, oranges, bananas and coconuts. However, the factors involved in constructing such an analysis would make it unfathomable to all but an expert. It may be better to limit the scope to a smaller number in order to make the results more tangible and expressible, and assume the effects of the other fruit on the chosen few. This approach is termed the use of *abstraction*, and while it leads to many criticisms of economic analysis, the results of an abstracted analysis can still be rewarding if the purposes of making economic models, explained earlier, are followed.

Allied to the concept of scope is detail. Detail is concerned with the numbers of actors involved. For example, should a family be treated as one or five actors? The answer clearly depends on the situation under consideration. Greater detail in an analysis has effects on the understanding of an analysis, while less detail may make the model invalid.

Likewise, emphasis reflects the aspects of the analysis that deserve special attention. When focusing on that aspect, the detail and the scope become increased in one area and decreased in all others. Emphasis is important in analysis that seeks to gain an understanding of a phenomenon.

All of the three previous concepts are brought together in the complexity of the model. However, complexity also includes the use of mathematics in the analysis and the flow of logic in the model. In general, a complex model is bad. It is important to bear in mind that complexity is a balance. If a model is too simple, it is easily disregarded; too complex, and it cannot be understood. One of the major skills in microeconomic analysis is determining the degree of complexity.

The types of microeconomic analysis

As was stated earlier, microeconomic analysis is an umbrella term for a range of analyses and models. The types of analysis performed can be summarized as:

- consumer choice
- social choice
- dynamic choice
- choice under uncertainty.

Each of these types of analysis has relevance to the following discussions on health economics. Therefore a brief description of each is justified. However, it is first necessary to introduce the market as a concept that underlies all of these analyses.

The market mechanism

A market is defined as a collection of buyers and sellers who interact, resulting in the possibility for exchange. It is worthwhile noting that a market is different from an industry, which is the term used for a group of firms that manufacture the same goods. Markets can be competitive or non-competitive. A competitive market has many buyers and sellers, so that no single buyer or seller has a significant impact on prices. Many of the natural resource markets, such as those of gold, tin and copper, approximate to competitive markets as there are many sellers and buyers. However, the world oil market is an example of a non-competitive market, as there are only a few producers who are able to fix prices – as exemplified by the oil crisis in the 1970s.

Markets operate according to the law of supply and demand. Sellers are willing to bring a certain volume of goods to market, depending on the price that consumers are willing to pay. The amount that consumers are willing to pay depends on the volume brought to market. According to the ideas introduced previously in the chapter, the net collective action of buyers and sellers produces an equilibrium. This equilibrium is usually depicted graphically as in Figure 1.1. The supply curve S tells us how much producers are willing to sell for each price. It curves upwards, as the higher the price, the more producers are willing to sell.

The demand curve D tells us how much buyers are willing to buy at a given price. It curves downwards, as the higher the price, the less consumers are likely to buy. Where the two curves cross is the equilibrium. This is the market price for the good. To understand why this is the equilibrium point, consider the point P_1 where the price is above the

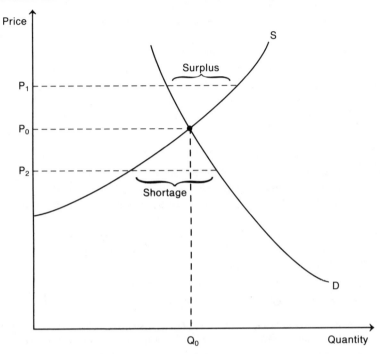

Figure 1.1 Supply and demand curves.

market price. Producers will bring to market more than they can sell, resulting in surplus. This surplus will cause the price to fall to the market price. If, on the other hand, goods are introduced below the market price, shortages of goods will result, leading to increased prices and more production. Market mechanisms – because of their inherent stability – also represent the most efficient way for goods and services to be distributed: the setting of prices achieved without the costs of an organization. In this manner, the market presents a stable exchange mechanism for consumers to make choices within.

Within the basic concepts of a market mechanism, the types of economic analysis are slotted. How they use the framework of the market differs with the analysis being considered.

Consumer choice analysis

This analysis is based on putting the preferences of the consumer as the central figure. The first step in performing this type of analysis is, therefore, to construct a model of consumer behaviour. The underlying idea of consumer choice is that a consumer will make choices so that he or she is satisfied with them. The expectation of satisfaction from a choice makes consumers have preferences as to what goods or services they buy. The objective of consumer choice is to examine these preferences and relate them to the external environment. In doing so, it relies on the consumer existing within a market and that the consumer has certain characteristics. These include the following:

- *Consumer choices and preferences are complete.* This implies that consumers are able to make choices over goods and are able to say they prefer one good to another. These preferences ignore costs at this stage.
- *Consumer preferences are transitive.* This means that if a consumer prefers a Rolls Royce to a Jaguar, and a Jaguar to a Ford, the consumer prefers a Rolls to a Ford. This assumption is very important as it ensures that choices are rational.
- *Consumers prefer more goods and services, to less.*

If the aim of consumer choice analysis is to describe the preferences of a consumer for goods, it becomes important to translate those preferences into choices under constraints. For example, the consumer prefers steak but can only afford hamburgers. Central to this application is *Marshallian demand*. Precise discussion about Marshallian demand is complex (interested readers are referred to the further reading list at the end of the chapter). However, at this point, some discussion of the concept is needed to facilitate discussion of the application of consumer choice in health economics.

According to Marshallian demand, a consumer will make choices such that the bundle of services consumed will be best according to preference limited by budgetary constraint. This definition implies that for every budgetary constraint, there will be a changing set of preferences expressed in a different bundle of goods and services purchased. By examining the bundles (often referred to as baskets) of services and goods purchased under different budgetary constraints, it becomes possible to estimate consumer preferences and understand the choices made. These estimations are performed by a variety of mathematical methods based on calculus, regression and correlation procedures.

Social choice

So far, our discussion has covered choice by single consumers in a variety of situations. This form of analysis, however, looks at the choice made by society. Instead of individual utility, the analysis of social choice is concerned with social outcomes. These outcomes usually embody two principles: equity and efficiency. Efficiency in this situation is defined according to two criteria: allocative and technical efficiency. These have been variously defined but, for the subject of our discussion, the simple definitions given below are provided.

1 *Allocative efficiency.* Have resources been allocated in such a way that the benefits to the population have been maximized?
2 *Technical efficiency or X efficiency.* Are the maximum benefits provided at minimum cost?

Allied to these concepts is equity. Equity reflects the fairness of the distribution of resources. Equity in health care is important, as we will see. However, for the current discussion we will treat equity as a single entity.

Central to the analysis of social choice is the *cost benefit analysis*. Cost benefit analysis plays a central role in health economics and is covered in greater detail later in the book.

Dynamic choice

So far, the analysis has treated choice as something that happens instantly. However, most choices are made through time, with consumers making repeated choices. The analysis of this situation and the determination of how preferences change is the aim of dynamic choice.

The prime example of dynamic choice is quality of life as a result of treatments, where consumers make a choice about the length and quality of life in the future based on treatments. Therefore, the discussion of dynamic choice is delayed until quality of life issues are addressed.

Choice under uncertainty

The discussion so far has assumed that what we choose is what we get. However, this is not always the case. Take, for example, the decision to spend money on an education. At the beginning, we are unsure of our abilities and those of our tutors. The satisfaction we derive from this education will only be apparent at the end of the course. However, we cannot postpone choice into the future. The decision to start work or go to college must be taken now. Analysis of choice under uncertainty is designed to look at this type of problem.

Nothing in the analysis of choice under uncertainty acts against anything we have stated so far; the decision to buy a second-hand car over a new car is still a choice that is based on our preferences and budgetary constraint. However, because we are uncertain about the state of the second-hand car, we have to adapt our analysis to accommodate the uncertainty.

The foundation of choice under uncertainty is *Von Neumann–Morgenstern Expected Utility*. This, like Marshallian demand, is a subject on which many textbooks are written and only the basic concepts are attempted here. Von Neumann–Morgenstern Expected Utility is based on the probability of achieving maximum satisfaction with a choice.

For example, we may express our satisfaction in terms of pounds (£). We are faced with an option to invest £100. The pay back is £100 with a probability of 0.5, £1000 with a probability of 0.1 and £50 with a probability of 0.3. We can represent this problem in a decision tree (Figure 1.2).

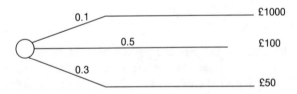

Figure 1.2 Decision tree.

The circular symbol at the beginning of the tree is known as the chance node. The value of the node is calculated by multiplying the value of the outcomes by the probabilities. In the example above, the node is valued at £165. This implies that on average for £100 invested we will get £165 in return. If we are comparing two or more choices, we can estimate the values of the expected outcomes by comparing the value of the chance nodes.

The analysis of choice under uncertainty is subject to all the restrictions of preference and choice in the consumer choice analysis.

Indeed, consumer choice is a special case of Von Neumann–Morgenstern Expected Utility where the probability of achieving maximum satisfaction is 1.

Choice under uncertainty is an important procedure in health economics, and the methods of analysis will be investigated in greater detail in a later chapter.

Does economics apply to health and health care?

It has frequently been argued that economics has little to do with health. Health is viewed as a basic right and should not be subjected to the cold, sterile world of health economics. It has to be acknowledged that this argument has some merit, especially where emergency medical treatment is concerned, as in this situation there is little time to conduct appraisals and make informed choices if lives are to be saved. However, not all treatments fit this image, and under non-emergency care, the efficient use of resources is desirable to allow the maximum number of individuals to benefit from health care. The basis of the efficient use of resources must be the making of informed choices by doctors and patients. Given the situation where economics can be applied to health and health care, the type of analysis performed will very much depend on the economic nature of health and health care.

The plot for the remainder of the book

The remainder of the book will focus on the types of analysis introduced so far and give examples of when these can be applied. The aim is to introduce the types of process undergone in as plain a manner as possible, using examples. The beginning of the process will be a review of market theory in health care, and it will then progress into consumer choice, choice under uncertainty, dynamic choice and social choice. Each chapter will review the 'pros' and 'cons' and add to the theory.

Further reading

Microeconomic theory, consumer choice, choice under uncertainty and dynamic choice:

Kreps DM (1990) *A course in microeconomic theory*, Chs 1–5. Hemel Hempstead, Harvester Wheatsheaf.

Social choice:

Pearce DW and Nash CA (1981) *The social appraisal of projects*. Basingstoke, Macmillan.

2 Institutional frameworks and health care

Key points from the previous chapter

Microeconomic analysis is centred around the prediction and explanation of the behaviour of actors in a system, often called a framework or institution. For an analysis to be valid, all these features must be present. There are various types of microeconomic analysis; consumer choice, social choice, dynamic choice and choice under uncertainty being the main ones. All of these types have the same founding principles.

The previous chapter has introduced the need for an institutional framework on which to base microeconomic analysis. The purpose of this chapter is to review the frameworks that exist in health care.

Market reform in health care

The development of markets in health care is a direct result of the reforms seen across Europe. These reforms inevitably have a basis in concerns about health care expenditure and look to microeconomic principles to increase the efficiency and productivity of health care producers, while maintaining equity. Despite the number of countries involved in market-style reforms in health care, debate continues on the appropriateness of the reforms and on the effects that market disciplines and competition have had on health care.

While it is common to talk about the market for health care, it is important to acknowledge that there is more than one type of market in health care. Health care markets differ in the nature of the incentives employed and in who the market pressure is applied to. However, they have common features in that they represent markets where competition is imperfect.

What is a market in health care?

All health care markets have the common feature that they represent a change from public bodies that are both the financier and provider of services. Instead, although the finance remains with the public body, the provision of services rests with a variety of independent, if not privately owned, services. In this manner, some degree of competition is introduced into the production of services. However, to a degree this competition is controlled – hence the term 'managed market', also called the internal or quasi-market. On the production side, there is less difference between conventional markets and quasi-markets as both involve competition between the providers of services. However, the prime motivation of health care producers may not be to maximize profits. As was stated in the previous chapter, as long as the providers of health care act as if they are profit maximizing, the conditions of the market still hold.

On the consumer side of the market there are significant differences between health care and conventional markets. In health care it is unusual for the consumer directly to express preferences in monetary terms. In health care preference is often expressed through another individual – the doctor – and even where preference is directly expressed, the expression will be in terms of using some services and not others, instead of in terms of price.

Why are markets the solution?

Market mechanisms are held to be the solution to the problems of expenditure in health care for a number of reasons. Health care markets can be broken down into two essential processes: the provision of care and the allocation of resources. Both of these processes are amenable to market models. The provision of care can be made more efficient by the use of market processes, as competition will lead to the stabilization of prices without expensive state interference. However, the application of market forces to resource allocation is more complex.

Resource allocation, i.e. the devotion of resources to projects and programmes, can be achieved by a spectrum of methods. In practice, these are not discrete but act as a continuum.

● *Market mechanisms.* This is allocation using the price mechanism 'You pays your money and you takes your choice'.

- *Technocratic allocation.* This is resource allocation mediated by professional groups, for example, clinicians.
- *Democratic allocation.* Resource allocation by public decision making.

The assumption behind markets in health care is that they will lead to a more efficient allocation of resources than will bureaucratic systems. The reasoning behind this is that bureaucratic systems offer little choice and therefore consumers have little power and, accordingly, public sector organizations act in the interests of the organization rather than in the interests of the individual. This is often manifest as departments attempting to maximize their budgets. In health care markets choice now resides with the consumers, or their proxies; if the services demanded are not available from a provider, the consumer can move demand. It is therefore in the best interest of the organization to listen to the consumer. Internal markets will only work, however, if choice is available. Not only must choice be available, but choice must also be informed and consumers must be able to make discernible choices, which is a dubious assumption in health care. In addition, even where choice exists, the power of individual consumers in health care may be small as the market is both diverse and fragmented.

Despite these possible problems, advocates of markets still argue that market mechanisms will lead to cost reduction. However, any improvement in value for money will depend on how the providers respond to the incentives to change their strategy. As public institutions have little incentive to manage profits, it is argued, why should quasi-markets reduce costs? Indeed, there are potential reasons for why a quasi-market may lead to increased costs. The costs of developing the infrastructure that can accurately bill purchasers, and the costs of advertising and tendering for work, are often quoted as reasons why quasi-markets may drive up costs. A more important factor may be the effect that competition has on labour costs. As there is only a finite amount of skilled labour, competition for employees may drive up costs.

A more fundamental criticism of health care markets lies in the definition of the market itself. The output of a health care market is difficult to define. Therefore there is the risk that the market may focus on the quality and quantity of the input. This would lead, for example, to the situation in which hospitals focus on the quality of their laboratories, or their consultants, rather than on the care that these facilities give. If there is a direct relationship between the quality of input and the outcome, this will not matter, but there is little evidence to support the relationship between the quality of a facility and the outcome of patients undergoing care.

The nature of internal markets and health care

As we have discussed, health care markets differ considerably from the perfect markets we have described in the previous chapter. In the health care market, consumers are rarely in the position of being able to make choices for themselves. Instead, a doctor often makes that choice. Also the actors in the system are often unable to make rational choices, as was explained previously. It is because of these factors that health care markets are imperfect. In order to ensure that the market results in some increase in efficiency and better resource allocation, rules are required within the market framework – hence the term 'internal markets'.

What defines an internal market?

Internal markets have three defining characteristics. First, they are modified conventional market structures. These modifications may be radical and are aimed at preventing market failure. The types of modification seen are regulations to control the entry of both purchasers and providers to the market, to control the profits of the organization in the market and to maintain access of the consumers to the market. The second feature of an internal market is that it contains structures allowing the management of the market to occur. These structures enable the market to be managed so that the wider social implications of a health care system can be maintained; for example, the NHS Executive (NHSE) is there to ensure that the principles of universal access to health care are maintained.

In order to achieve this role, the NHSE has certain powers:

- to control entry and exit to the market
- to maintain services in equity, availability, access and quality
- to review prices
- to manage incentives to providers
- to review the determinants of population health
- to define efficiency and efficiency gains.

The NHSE has equivalents in other market reforms of health care. In some countries, the role is performed by the Ministry of Health (e.g. France) or semi-independent bodies (e.g. The Netherlands).

The third characteristic of an internal market is the limitation of trading within that market. So health care markets only trade in health care.

The points above are fundamental to an internal market, although in practice there are other features included: all internal markets offer choice of providers, separate purchasers and providers, permit the cash limitation of public expenditure and can accommodate both public and private ownership of health care providers.

The creation of internal markets, in addition to adding the possibility of competitors, also provides the potential to offer a wide range of policy options within a single structure. An example of this is the Dutch reforms, where both social insurance, private insurance and internal markets are being employed.

In practice, there are five variations of internal market:

1 compulsory private insurance
2 social insurance
3 primary care purchasing
4 competitive bidding
5 managed competition.

In order to further the discussion, it is important to understand a little about each system.

Compulsory private insurance

Compulsory private insurance-based internal markets have been in operation in the USA for some time and have also been proposed in Guernsey. Under this system, all citizens would have to purchase private health insurance, the government contracting with the insurers to purchase cover for those who cannot afford to do so (Medicaid and Medicare in the USA). The insurer guarantees a universal minimum level of cover at a price reflecting the subscriber's income. The insurers themselves are closely regulated, as are the providers of care.

Under the Guernsey proposals, entry and exit to the market would be state controlled, as would prices and quality. This is a fundamental difference from the situation in the USA, where quality and prices are left to the insurers.

Social insurance

In northern Europe (Belgium, The Netherlands and Germany, for example) social insurance models are the basis for a long standing internal market. Health insurance in these countries is compulsory, public bodies purchasing insurance for those who cannot afford it. However, premiums paid are regulated by the state, rather than by individual companies. Patient, state and employer all contribute to the payment of premiums. Therefore, virtually global coverage for a minimum range of services is guaranteed. The purchasers of health care are non-specialized, commercial sickness funds, organized either geographically or along trade union or religious lines. The cost of the services offered is fixed by negotiation. Private insurers and sick funds also offer 'top up' insurance to purchase a wider range of services.

Market entry is regulated by accreditation. In this way, the quantity of services is maintained. Management structures therefore control quality and price.

Primary doctor purchasing

Primary care-led purchasing has been introduced as part of the NHS reforms as GP fundholding, although similar experiments have been tried in Sweden and Russia. It is based on the role of the primary care team as the gatekeepers to secondary or hospital care.

Under this system, medical care is purchased by clinicians from cash-limited budgets allocated to them by the management structure. Primary medical care may be purchased from the same budget (Russia) or a separate budget (UK). In theory, every patient has the right to register with a primary care physician, so the right to universal care is maintained.

Secondary care providers are regulated by the willingness of the physician to refer patients. Although public funded hospitals predominate, the range of provider can include charities and voluntary sectors.

Price and quality are regulated by negotiations between purchaser and provider. Disputes between the purchasers and providers are usually handled by a management structure, for example the NHSE.

Competitive bidding

The reforms introduced into the Swedish health care system and the competitive tendering process in the NHS are both examples of the competitive bidding type of internal market. Providers bid competitively to provide services to a management structure. The purchaser of the service decides the specification and the quality standards. In this way, competition between providers can be planned, and market entry is controlled by the management structure.

Managed competition

Managed competition is typified by the Dutch reforms and is a focus for the US reforms. In managed competition, relations between purchasers and providers are managed by a layer of regulatory bodies. This is done so that the equity of health care can be maintained and the purchasers of health care can offer a guaranteed basic range of health care available to all, irrespective of the current health status of a population or individual. To spread the financial risk, it is necessary to either create large pools of purchasers or to ensure that there is adequate access to a large risk pool. This system does not exclude individuals from being compulsorily insured, with the state providing coverage for those who cannot afford it.

Managed competition leaves open the policy question of contributions paid by individuals to the cost of cover and the levels of private insurance. The intermediate bodies can surcharge purchase to compensate for bias in insurance.

The entry of providers into the market is closely regulated by accreditation. The management of incentives is left to the intermediate body. Purchasing may also be regulated to providers offering certain safeguards, e.g. diagnostic-related groups (DRG)-based contracts.

How do internal markets in health care work?

The models of the internal market make the management of a health system achievable, by focusing on restriction of competition and incentives. The keys to these incentives are the payment mechanisms.

All types of internal market have payment to providers for incurred expenses. These payments have a variety of features: standard tariffs (payment of a fee for service or cost per case), capitation, block payments, cost and volume payments. All internal markets make use of these payment mechanisms to a greater or lesser degree. For example, in the competitive bidding NHS internal market, a move from block contracts to cost per case is the norm for DHAs, while GP fundholders more frequently use cost per case. Project payments, payments for health promotion and research and development, are used commonly by DHAs, but rarely by fundholders.

The incentive system offered by payments within regulated markets is well described. Cost per case payment acts as an incentive to maximize the number of patients and the cost per patient. Capitation payments act to increase patient numbers and minimize cost. Cost and volume contracts act in much the same manner but incentives vary with the wording of the contract. Block contracts have a complex incentive system, most authorities stating that they minimize numbers and service quality. The payment incentives give the health care providers pseudo-commercial reasons to maximize charges and minimize costs. The effect of incentives in the internal market are not as acute when markets are growing, when the evidence is that quality becomes a major feature.

In primary care-led purchasing, there are two additional sets of incentives to consider. The first of these is for the provider of care, who has to meet the GPs' demands for quality, as well as those of the patient; these two sets of demands may differ considerably. The other set of incentives is that of primary care doctors. GPs have their own personal incentives, which may make them seek to provide services for themselves – a further threat to the institutional providers.

The role of the private sector in internal health care markets

So far in this discussion we have focused on the incentives facing public bodies and institutions. However, the private sector has a significant role in health care markets. All five models of the regulated market permit private bodies to play a major role in health care provision. Indeed, private enterprise is essential to the managed competition and compulsory insurance models of health care markets, although not to the other models. Regardless of ownership, it has been argued that the internal market will make all providers of care act to maximize profit as:

• providers are competing for income
• reinvestment is key and provides competitive services
• reinvestment comes from retained profits or borrowing.

The strength of the force to maximize profits varies between the various models deployed. This has the effect that the role of the private sector also varies. In the competitive bidding process, such as is employed in the UK, the profit motive can be reduced by incorporating service developments into the bidding structure. Such initiatives are seen in the capital resource allocation working party as the revenue of capital schemes. More recently, we have seen the use of capital grants both to stimulate providers and to provide for service developments.

The power of private providers will also depend on the type of competitive development. For example, in the UK, GPs, although they are independent practitioners, face a monopoly in both the purchasing and provision of health care that weakens the power of private providers.

The role of the purchaser

In addition to allowing significant private input, at the risk of market failure, regulated markets also introduce a new player into health care provision – the purchaser.

Purchasers play a larger role in internal market development. How they behave, however, depends very much on the incentives they have and how these are used. The role of purchasers also depends on the objectives of the market. For example, in primary care-led purchasing, the objectives are the achievement of satisfactory patient care while minimizing the cost and maintaining primary care physician control over the process. In contrast, managed competition centres on guaranteeing levels of provider reimbursement while maintaining access to care. These differences explain why in Holland most purchasers are commercial while in the UK the purchasers are state controlled. Where commercial purchasers exsist, there is the tendency to maximize the number of subscribers, possibly to the detriment of non-subscribers' health.

The power of purchasers will also depend on the degree of fragmentation. This has the effect of increasing the number of sources of provider income. Therefore, for effective management structures in internal markets management structures must:

• have a recognized legal or regulatory function, possibly backed up by strong purchasers

- develop purchasers with sufficiently strong bargaining power
- be an adequate audit and monitoring system.

While these three criteria hold for most internal markets, other features are essential in primary care-led purchasing. Here purchaser power is often a function of practice size. Therefore practices are often size limited.

The problems of health care markets

The development of an internal market implies that some problems will occur. The problems with internal markets are termed 'market failures'. This term implies either that the market fails to protect those in need or that purchasers and providers go bankrupt on a large scale. The type of failure will very much depend on the structure of the market and the financial incentives and perversities on offer.

Internal markets can be very sensitive to the behaviour of incentives. A good example is the effect of controls on polyclinic referrals in Leningrad. This had the effect of a massive increase in emergency referrals, which nearly brought the market to its knees.

Internal markets are also very sensitive to any cost pressures applied. Where commercial pressures predominate, for example, respite and chronic disease management tends to suffer. Another form of cost pressure is internal costs, often termed transaction costs. It has been argued that internal markets may fail owing to the high transaction costs associated with them. It has been estimated that the transaction costs associated with primary care-led purchasing in the UK may amount to £85 000 per practice per annum.

A fourth reason why it is agreed that internal markets may fail is owing to the presence of moral hazard or provider-induced demand, where providers are able to treat patients without control. This is known to be greatest in the competitive bidding and primary care types of market.

A fifth type of market failure can result from competing incentives. An example is in the UK market, where purchasers are encouraged to seek as much activity as they can.

There are a range of suggested managerial solutions to the problem caused by internal market failure. These vary with not only the type of market, but also the degree to which they interfere with the functioning of the market. The most common ways of dealing with market failure are given below.

- *Tactical variation.* Purchasing by the management structure, rather than the purchasers, of services which are prone to market failure. An example is the long stay care of the mentally ill, where the NHS executive has retained power.
- *Market development.* By bringing in external market players, market failure can be prevented. An example is the use of capital grants in the UK market.
- *Variation in market regulations.* By changing the regulations for entry and exit, for example, market failure can be prevented.

Conclusion

This chapter has introduced the first essential element of microeconomic analysis in health care: that of the framework or institution. It has shown that it is possible for more than one framework to exist and has suggested five models for consideration. It has also served to highlight the actors within the various types of framework and give some idea of their relative importance. How economic models are constructed to explain the behaviour of each actor is the subject of subsequent chapters.

Further reading

Satman RB and Von Otter C (eds) (1995) *Implementing planned markets in health care.* Milton Keynes, Open University Press.

3 Health care as an economic commodity

Key points from the previous chapter

Health care markets are institutions that permit the exchange of resources for health care. There are several types of health care market, each with unique features. However, all have the separation of purchasers and providers.

So far, we have covered the basic concepts of microeconomic analysis and introduced the framework of health care markets. Before proceeding to develop analytical methods for health care, it is important to understand how economists view it.

The characteristics of an economic good or service

Goods in economic terms are the result of resource exchange; they represent the output and outcomes of market behaviour. In economics, goods are of two types: private goods and public goods. A private good is one that is solely for the use of the economic actor. However, a public good is one that, once sold, cannot be exclusively used by one individual and is open to society. A garden is a good example. If an individual landscapes a garden, his neighbours benefit from the scented flowers and the visual effect. Public goods are very important as they are frequently the concern of government policy. Policy towards public goods acts to ensure the fair distribution of the good across the spectrum of society. Some aspects of health care behave as if they were public goods, immunization against infection being an example. The reduction of infectious diseases in the community by vaccination reduces the chances of an unvaccinated individual catching the disease – this is a public good effect.

Health care as an economic good

Individuals do not willingly enter the health care market. They do not go in search of health care. Instead, the individual seeks health. In response to the demand for health, the consumer receives health care. This complex relationship is at the centre of the economic behaviour of health care. Therefore, the investigation of health care as an economic good must begin with a discussion about the relationship between health and health care.

A definition of health

Health is often defined as a lack of illness. This is not a satisfactory definition as illness is defined as the absence of health. In medical practice, health is defined in terms of the absence of physical or mental disturbance. These disturbances are taken as a reaction to an external stimulus. This definition is also problematical as it relies on methods of measuring the presence of a disturbance. In an attempt to solve the problems, the World Health Organization (WHO) has described health as 'A complete state of physical, emotional and social well-being, and not merely the absence of disease and infirmity'. This cumbersome definition is the beginning of all discussions regarding the nature of health care. However, on closer inspection, it is apparent that this definition is unworkable in economic practice, where it is the individual's preference for health, rather than an absolute standard, that matters. Therefore, economists tend to use the medical definition of health and define the effectiveness and efficiency of health care in terms of returning the individual to a relative state of health, as characterized by the absence of symptoms and signs. Accordingly, the individual's preference for this state of health is measured against that of the presence of illness.

The economic nature of health care

Given this definition, the economic nature of health care is an investigation of the relationship between investments in health care – inputs – and the improvement in health – outcomes. Hence health economics must concern itself with a discussion of the likely effectiveness of any intervention in improving health. In this situation, the sources of information about health and health care are the most valuable.

The sources of health-related data

The usual source of health-related data is national records. However, these are only on a population level, and it is often unclear why changes in mortality and life expectancy occur. Therefore most of the information about health and health-related events comes from epidemiological studies. There are several types of study, each of which varies in its capacities to examine effective interventions. Most rigorous is the randomized controlled clinical trial, in which patients are randomly allocated to receive the treatments under study. This type of trial is widely acknowledged as the 'gold standard' in terms of the reliability of information. Next to the randomized trial in terms of information value comes the cohort study, in which groups of individuals are subject to treatments. Last come the descriptive studies. For a detailed discussion on clinical trial methodology, a reference is given at the end of the chapter.

The foundation of all these types of trial is the measurement of health. Health may be measured as a change in a biochemical indicator – the enzyme amylase in pancreatitis, for example. Alternatively, health may be measured using a symptom score. This method is common in rheumatology. Health status may also be measured using a scoring system that reflects total health, often termed holistic health. Whatever the methods employed, these changes must, from an economic viewpoint, be attributable to the costs and benefits of health care, and preferences should be expressed for the perceived changes.

A preference for health care?

The requirement for the description of preferences in health economic analysis is problematical as we are left asking, 'whose preferences?'. Health care is a highly political activity, and health care changes may be influenced by the political process rather than a drive for health. In an attempt to resolve some of these issues, the study of health care involves a unique abstraction (abstraction in economics was introduced in Chapter 1). Instead of studying health outcomes directly, health economists study health care outputs and relate these back to health. In this manner, health care trends can be studied in the absence of political inference on health. This abstraction, while solving the problem, puts a different emphasis on health care economics. Health care economics can only be a consideration in health care decision making, rather than the major deciding factor. This is an important message, to which we will return many times.

Who's preference?

The difficulty in expressing preferences in health care is compounded by the way in which health care is delivered. The decision to seek health care, and what health care to seek, may not be the choice of the patient. In most health care systems, the doctor decides what health care, and how much, that patient will receive. In economics terms, this is known as an *agency relationship*. The agency relationship has important consequences when the optimum use of resources is considered, as the ultimate consumer of health care – the patient – will have only a limited idea about the benefit that will be received by following the doctor's advice. This seriously flaws much of the microeconomic theory we have discussed in Chapter 1 and places limitations on the use of economic analysis.

The impact of preference

The problems in the consideration of preference in health care have little impact on the processes of normative analysis of health care. The aim of normative analysis is to provide information to aid decisions. The fact that the final consumer may not be the decision maker makes little difference to the analysis. The agency relationship, however, has a large impact if positive analysis is considered. The determination of market prices, as we have seen, is dependent upon informed consumers making choices for themselves. This is clearly not the situation in health care. For this reason, the application of positive methods is limited in health care; this is the subject of the following chapter.

The existence of an agency relationship in health care has further effects. First, it is important to appreciate that health is not produced solely by health care. Changes in social conditions can have a profound influence on the health of an individual. A second consideration stemming from this point is that not all health care results in health. This effect distorts the demand for health care and can lead to the situation in which the perceived demand for health – as felt by a consumer – and the actual gain in health are considerably at variance.

Finally, it should be remembered that health has very little value *per se*; health only has value when it enables us to do something else. In addition to the value of health only in use, individuals differ in how they value their health. These considerations make the demand for health care a very poor proxy for the demand for health.

The effect of the agency relationship will clearly depend on the type of care being administered. In the case of sudden life-threatening illness, decisions about the course of treatment taken will rest more heavily on doctors and nurses, rather than on patients. In general, the more trivial the condition, the more the patient will be able to express a preference.

The agency relationship implies that the consumption of health care resources, by the doctor, and the utility or satisfaction gained from health care, by the patient, are disassociated. This raises the issue of *property rights* in health care. Property rights is an economic term that relates to the behavioural relationship between individuals arising from the existence of things and relating to their use. They determine an individual's rights to use and consume resources. In traditional economic thinking, the property rights of health care, i.e. the right of the individual to use health care, rests with the individual. The preceding discussion indicates that this may not be the case. This situation raises questions about the use of the concept of utility (as was discussed in Chapter 1) in health care.

Other problems with utility

There are other reasons to doubt the use of utility in health care. More specifically, there are concerns about equity. Equity in health care can be likened to justice. Equity can be viewed in at least four ways. These are:

- *entitlement* (in which individuals are entitled to their fair share of health resources based on the amount they have contributed)
- *utilitarian* (which is about the efficient use of resources, implying a form of negative equity as it concerns itself with the most good for the most people)
- *maximin* (the maximum benefit for the least advantaged)
- *egality* (perhaps best defined as equal health for all).

The role of equity in health economics

Health economists often take the view that equity is a countervailing force to efficiency. They consider it as a conscious departure for the pursuit of maximum efficiency in the interest of a more equal distribution of health. The concept of equity features very large in current health economic literature, particular attention being paid to the combination of equity and efficiency.

However, there is an inherent problem with this approach. The *Pareto Principle* is the founding principle of welfare economics. It concerns the distribution of welfare, in which health is included, in terms of the utility of one set of individuals compared to another when both are in different circumstances. Equity, on the other hand, is concerned with different individuals in the same set of circumstances. Therefore many of the methods developed concerning welfare economics cannot be applied to health where equity is concerned.

The two areas in which equity in health care is of particular concern are the effects of sociodemographics and geography. These two effectively embody the major concerns about equity. First, there is the effect of so-called vertical equity, i.e. the unequal treatments of people who are not equal, for example the treatment of individuals with different health conditions, such as pneumonia and influenza. The concept of vertical equity involves equal treatment for equal need. Second, there is the concern of horizontal equity, concerning the equal treatment of individuals with the same condition who differ in geography or social class. While these concepts are easy to espouse, they are very difficult to put in practice.

The concerns of policy makers for equity should not be underestimated. One of the reasons for the foundation of the NHS was the concern about the unequal availability of health care because of social class and geography. It can be argued that the NHS has not been successful in this aim, but it must nonetheless be agreed that it remains a goal.

One of the major problems in discussing equity, however, is how to measure it. Central to this issue is the definition of need. We have already discussed in previous sections the concepts of need in economic terms. How are these reflected in clinical practice?

The determination of need in different geographic and social areas has, in the past, relied on the measurement of proxies for illness. These have featured the standardized mortality ratio as the most used measurement. While this is a useful measurement for mortality, it does not reflect all sickness or morbidity found in a community. It therefore ignores the concept of equal access to therapy for equal need, important in the measurement of horizontal equity. Equity considerations have therefore largely focused on equity of input, not equity of outcomes.

The interdependency of health economic utility and equity

It is often assumed that, in making economic decisions, man is selfish. The importance of incorporating equity into health care, is that it allows for individuals to make choices that are not completely altruistic. This can best be described as the concept of *caring eternality*. An eternality in economics is a factor that changes the consumption and patterns of provision of a good but does not affect the price. In this way, caring may distort the values of health care.

The interaction of equity and utility has been examined via a series of philosophical frameworks. These have focused on what framework should be adopted. The suggestions for the gains in equity that should be traded against utility include:

- equal access for equal need
- equal *per capita* spending
- equal use of services
- equal health.

The most frequently proposed example is equal access for equal need, although in adopting this stance, little emphasis is placed on the effectiveness of the care offered.

A word about ethics

It often appears that the ethics employed in economics and medical ethics are at loggerheads. The reasons for this lie in the bases for the ethical viewpoints, the fundamental point of disagreement being the way in which priorities are set. There are considerable worries among medical ethicists about the use of cost benefit analysis and in particular the practice of placing a monetary value on human life. The concern is that, by using these methods, choice will be made on financial reasoning, rather than health. There are certainly concerns about applying cost benefit analysis to health care, which will be made clear in the next chapter. However, it has been argued that in a situation of scarcity, it is impossible not to place a value on human life. A further tenet is that by making choices explicit, their true ethical value can be evaluated.

The impact of medical ethics in economics is made complex by the agency relationship that exists between doctor and patient. However, there are considerable concerns about extending this relationship into prioritizing health care between groups of patients, for example the young versus the old, in relation to the power the doctor holds over his patient. The application of personal values to decisions without a framework could lead to great inequities in the system.

Another area of concern is the conflict of equity and utilitarian values. Economists, as explained above, seek maximum efficiency but are prepared to offset efficiency against equity. Concerns are expressed among medical ethicists that the pursuit of this system leads to a situation of marginalization of the incurable and chronically sick. However, it is to be remembered that the role of economics is to inform choice, rather than to make choices.

Conclusion

Health care is a complex economic commodity and it has not been possible in this chapter to visit all of its aspects. However, the nature of health care, and how it is provided, shapes the types of health care analyses that are performed. The role of equity in health care is still evolving and will continue to be one of the major discussion points in health. Of particular concern is its role in the development of analysis to reflect the changes in primary care – where drugs are used across all ages and boundaries.

How these considerations are used in health economic analysis will be the subject of the remainder of the book.

Further reading

Brown CV and Jackson PM (1991) *Public sector economics*. Blackwell, Oxford.
Pocock SJ (1990) *Clinical trials*. John Wiley & Sons, Chichester.

4 Consumer choice in health care

Key points from the previous chapter

The economic nature of health and health care is complex. It is reflected in a demand for health being met by a supply of health care. In addition, the agency relationship brings into question the concept of utility in health care analysis. For this reason the scope of analysis using microeconomic methods is limited. This is more evident in the practice of positive analysis, rather than in normative analysis.

Our foray into health economic analysis has so far stressed the limitation of many of the analytical types. Despite the limitations, however, consumer choice analysis still has an important role in the determination of consumer behaviour in purchasing insurance and other activities not related to health care but which are health producing, for example sports. In this way, health and health care can be considered to have similarity to any other capital investment. This implies that actors are making an investment of resources now for some future benefit.

The aim of this chapter is to provide a non-mathematical description of consumer choice and to indicate its uses. Those more interested in the process are invited to look at the further reading. The chapter also aims to introduce the important arguments in consumer choice that have a major bearing when the other forms of analysis are introduced.

Consumer choice analysis

As was stated in Chapter 1, consumer choice analysis seeks to look at the behaviour of economic actors in a competitive market place. The actors it looks at include individual consumers and also the firms that support the production of goods and services that consumers purchase. The relationship between production and demand is symbolized by the supply and demand curve. The previous sections have also highlighted the fact that the nature of health care means that not all assumptions and abstractions made in consumer choice are valid.

Factors influencing consumer choice in health care

We have already discussed some of the problems in consumer choice analysis that make the application of this analytical framework limited. These factors include the agency relationship and the ability to make rational choice, as characterized by informed choice and the principle of transitivity. However, even within the areas where consumer choice analysis is widely accepted, there are some restrictions on the type of analysis. This is as the unique nature of health and health care modifies the relationship between consumer and supplier of health care. These are best looked at in terms of factors influencing demand and factors related to behaviour.

Demand factors

The factors that influence demand include the following.

- The consumer is seeking health rather than health care.
- Consumers are not only the receivers of health care but, by their actions, also act as producers of health by investing in health improving activities.
- Health has no value – except in use. You cannot go to a supermarket and buy it by the kilo.
- Health lasts for more than one period, i.e. if you invest in health today, it is still there tomorrow. Also health does not depreciate: health today is not worth 5% less tomorrow.

All of these features impact on consumer choice on investing in health and, because of these consumer choices in health care, are often referred to as the *household production of health*. This implies that in order to invest to produce health, consumers will sacrifice their leisure time and income to increase their capital stock of health.

Behavioural factors

The ability to invest in health, and the demand for health, is not just a function of leisure time and income, however, as behavioural factors have an influence. Central among these factors are the age and education of the actors concerned, as well as the behavioural aspects of income.

Age

As an actor ages, his stock of health declines naturally, and the rate of decline increases with age. This situation would imply that the demand for health care would increase with age – which we know to be the case. However, the models would also imply that with increasing age, actors will devote a greater proportion of their income to health care and health-related investments – at a time when total income is declining.

Education

The range of investments available to an actor will depend on education for two reasons. First, higher-educated individuals are more likely to be higher earners. Second, the more educated actors are likely actively to seek health investments. Education is therefore a demand modifier, like age. Increasing educational status therefore, like age, increases demand. The effects on the proportion of income are different, however, owing to the higher earning status of individuals.

Wage

We have already hinted that increasing wage drives demand and that wage correlates to age and education, but wage has an effect on its own in that being a high earner motivates individuals to stay that way, so they can earn more.

The effect of demand and behaviour on consumer choice

The overall effect of both demand and behavioural factors is that no general equilibrium can be described. Instead consumer choice relies on the description of partial equilibria, where only some of the factors are taken into account. These partial equilibria are unique to the analytical situation. This makes it impossible to say for certain that if tax increases, for example, the consumption of health care will decline. This contrasts with the analysis of other situations where reproducible equilibria are sought.

Despite the lack of a general equilibrium resulting from consumer choice analysis of health care, however, some conclusions can be reached. It is clear that income and health investments are closely linked, i.e. *the willingness to pay for health investments equates with the ability to pay*. This is an important conclusion. It implies that if health care were to be left solely to market mechanisms, the distribution of health care would be skewed towards those who could afford it. As health is considered a basic right, it is up to governmental intervention to correct this tendency by policy decisions. These policy decisions were touched on in Chapters 2 and 3.

The problem with willingness to pay also explains why the use of consumer choice analysis is so limited. It implies that the satisfaction with health care is a function not of the health care goods on offer, but of the ability to buy them. Therefore the equilibrium described is more a function of wages than illness.

Other considerations in consumer choice

In addition to the factors that influence actors directly, there are other influences in consumer choice analysis. These revolve around time and information.

When an actor is investing in health or health care, time appears to be a major deciding criterion. The important period is the time from investment to pay-off. In general, investments today are benefits forgone today. This aspect of health investment is very important when social choices are considered. Therefore, while acknowledging that the investment period is important, and benefits received tomorrow will have to be discounted for the value placed on resources today, a more detailed discussion is delayed until the next chapter.

Information in health care

The other major factor influencing health investments is information. In the introductory section we stipulated that, for consumer choice analysis to be valid, the actors must be fully informed and possess all the information necessary to make choices. We have further said that this scenario may not be relevant to health care. What is the nature of this information mismatch?

Mismatches in economic information are termed *asymmetries*. Asymmetries of information occur in health care for a variety of reasons.

First, the patient may not know what illness is present, nor for that matter may the doctor. Second, the patient may not know whether the doctor is giving appropriate therapy. Finally, and perhaps most importantly, is the fact that doctors and patients conceal knowledge from each other. This is particularly true of patients who may conceal life-style factors that increase their chances of disease.

Information asymmetries have a major impact on health care investments. In insurance, asymmetric information, in terms of the patient concealing known facts, leads to the situation of adverse selection. This implies that the insurance company will have to increase premiums to all of its members to cover those who may be concealing information. Asymmetric information also has a major impact on the demand for health care. We have already mentioned that most health care is given via an agency relationship. If the doctor, when acting as an agent, gives unneeded treatment the information gap will mean that the patient is unaware of the excess. This can lead to the phenomenon of supplier-induced demand (SID). SID is a major concern to health care planners, and it is postulated that some medical practice variations are due to SID.

From these discussions, health care acts as a *reputation* good. We have already seen that health care has some aspects of a public good; however, a reputation good implies that some of its exchange properties rely on the reputation of the person giving the care. In this manner, institutions can be seen as a good institution or a bad institution. I vividly remember my grandmother refusing to enter the local high-technology hospital because people died there; instead she died in the cottage hospital down the road. It is the same with individual practitioners. These perceptions often have little foundation in information, yet they act as though they were information. Therefore they contribute to the problem of asymmetric information in health care. This is important, as individuals investing in health may choose to invest in a not-for-profit organization rather than a profit-based group purely because one operates not for profit, so is perceived as better.

The impact of the problem

Before going any further with the development of information problems in health care, it is important to size the problem. The information asymmetries seen in health care are no worse than those seen in other areas, for instance the used car market or personal accident insurance. However, the unique nature of health and health care focuses the mind on these problems. These problems can be overcome by the careful use of accreditation, physician panels and ethical constraints. It is perhaps unwise to state, as many commentators do, that in difficulties with health care, information and information asymmetry preclude the development of competition in health care.

Applying consumer choice in health care

So far we have explored the factors influencing consumer choice. These are important because, as we stressed earlier, each type of analysis we do is related to the others. Therefore consumer choice restraints have a major impact on social choice analysis. However, this still begs the question of how and why consumer choice is applied. Consumer choice analysis is important in the development of insurance. Many health care systems rely on the co-payment by insurers of health care expenses. Indeed, one of the major discussions about the NHS is how long it can survive without co-payments.

The existence of co-payments has a major impact on the demand for health care and the quality of services delivered. An important concept in this discussion is the elasticity of the demand for health care. The elasticity of a good is defined as the effect on demand of a change in unit price. Experimental evidence suggests that there is some change by the consumers of health care in response to co-payment charges, although the true significance of this finding is unclear (see Further reading). Instead, health care is income driven, and changes to income have a major effect. Insurers, and other agencies that pay co-payments, have the problem of deciding a premium for their services. This is clearly a difficult task as the size of premium depends more on the population served than on the demand for health care. Therefore the description of supply and demand curves relative to income is important in determining the level of co-payment.

Another use for consumer-based analysis is the development of managed care. Managed care is a misquoted and misunderstood term. In this text, we will define managed care as a system that seeks to manage the clinical and financial risks associated with health care. The mechanisms by which managed care companies seek to manage risk include the sharing of risks with providers of care and the pharmaceutical companies. The sharing of risk has major impacts on pharmaceutical profits and cash flows and the description of supply and demand curves in this situation is important in determining the equilibrium price under managed care situations.

The key to both of these situations is a description of the demand for health care by actors under varying situations. The partial equilibrium models produced by consumer choice analysis enable decision makers to set a price and volume of services provided.

Conclusion

This chapter has introduced consumer choice analysis. Although the use of consumer choice is limited where it is used in setting co-payments and in risk sharing, it is an important source of information. The limitations of consumer choice analysis have an impact on the remaining analytical procedures.

Further reading

Folland S, Goodman AC and Stano M (1993) Supply and demand. Part 2 of *The economics of health and health care*, pp. 99–223. Macmillan, Basingstoke.

5 Social analysis and dynamic choice

> *Key points from the previous chapter*
>
> *The previous chapter introduced the basic concepts of consumer choice analysis. These points are important as they have a major bearing on the other types of analysis performed in health care. The chapter also highlighted the uses of consumer choice analysis and how the restrictions placed on the analysis of consumer choice influences health care.*

In our critique of health economics, we have so far explored the relationships between the price of health care and the amount that individuals are prepared to invest in it. However, this subject is not at the centre of health care decision makers' minds. In all health care systems, resources are scarce, and decisions must be made on how to spend them in order to gain most benefit, i.e. there are normative questions. In providing information to assist the decision maker the economist is concerned with a different set of relationships, that of efficiency and equity and time. For this reason social choice and dynamic choice in health care are linked and best considered together.

The social analysis of projects in economic terms is the realm of cost benefit analysis. Cost benefit analysis is often surrounded by an aura of mystique but quite simply it implies that the benefits and costs of projects being considered will have to be measured. The costs and benefits will also have to be judged in accordance with who pays and who benefits, before being considered alongside the alternatives.

The basis of cost benefit analysis

Cost benefit analysis is an umbrella term for a group of related methods that are used to assess the value of costs and benefits of alternative treatments. These methods are cost benefit analysis (confusingly!), cost

Table 5.1 The types of cost benefit analysis

Type of study	Measurement and valuation of costs	Identification of outcome	Measurement and valuation of outcome
Cost minimization	Pounds	Assumed to be identical	None
Cost effectiveness	Pounds	Single unit for all alternatives considered, but of different magnitudes	Natural units, e.g. lives saved
Cost benefit	Pounds	Single or multiple outcomes not common to alternatives	Pounds
Cost utility	Pounds	Single or multiple outcomes not common between alternatives	Quality adjusted life years or equivalent

effectiveness analysis, cost minimization and cost utility. Each of these has features that tailor its use to certain situations (Table 5.1).

Cost benefit analysis values all costs and benefits in monetary units. It therefore places values in terms of pounds on features such as human life. The convention in cost benefit analysis is that all costs and benefits are included, inclusive of non-health care-related costs and benefits. This form of analysis is usually performed where allocative efficiency questions are being answered. This contrasts with *cost effectiveness analysis*, which is usually used where technical efficiency is being addressed. Cost effectiveness analysis is concerned with the measurement of outcomes in natural units, for example reduction in blood pressure or changes in cholesterol. These are compared with the costs of achieving these changes. By convention, the costs only include health care-associated costs.

Both *cost minimization* and *cost utility* analyses are really a variation of cost effectiveness analysis. Cost minimization is an analysis in which the costs of obtaining a given outcome are compared. Hence all alternatives must have identical outcomes. Cost utility analysis, in contrast, measures outcomes in terms of the satisfaction that patients have with the outcome of therapy. Cost utility analysis also encompasses the concepts of dynamic choice, as patients are asked to value outcomes in the future. Both of these methods may address either technical or allocative questions and may use the full range of costs.

All of these analyses have features in common. All rely on the identification of costs and the quantification of those costs. However, the methods handle outcomes differently. Regardless of the methodology, the evaluation is seeking to answer questions about the value of performing a programme relative to other expenditure.

Some important limitations

As in all forms of economic analysis, there are limitations on the situations in which cost benefit analysis can be used. Before even considering an analysis, some basic questions must be asked.

1 *Does the proposed treatment work?* Evidence of effectiveness should be supplied. In general, this should be as robust as possible.
2 *Can it work in practice?* Can the proposed treatment be delivered in such a way that it is acceptable to patients, so they will use the service offered?
3 *Will it reach those in need?* Is the programme accessible to those who need it?

Unless a new therapy and all the comparison treatments can give positive answers to all of these questions, an analysis should not be performed. The need to perform an analysis also relies on the type of data that are available. Cost benefit analysis can only be performed when information is available about both the costs and benefits of an intervention. Where costs are available without any outcome measurement, the only type of analysis that is legitimate is a cost analysis.

When to undertake an analysis

The decision to undertake a cost benefit analysis should not be easily reached. Cost benefit analyses are time-consuming and problematical and should not be undertaken lightly. Reviewing the literature, it is apparent that many analyses are undertaken unnecessarily, yet it is quite easy to determine when to do an analysis (Figure 5.1).

		Costs	
		Increased	Decreased
Outcomes	Better	Needed	Dominant
	Worse	Indefensible	Needed

Figure 5.1 When to perform a cost benefit analysis.

It is indefensible to perform a cost benefit analysis when outcomes are worse and costs are higher. Where outcomes are better and costs lower, this is a dominant strategy. Cost benefit analysis is important when outcomes are better and costs higher, or outcomes worse and costs lower.

It is important to re-state that in performing an analysis, the economist is not seeking to make decisions but to inform the decision making process. Where outcomes and costs are lower, the decision maker may decide that this is not ethically viable and this analysis should not be performed.

The process of cost benefit analysis

Cost benefit analysis can be divided into a number of stages. These can be usefully thought of as providing a sequential classification of events in an analysis.

Specifying the alternatives for appraisal

Since the objective of the analysis is to determine the most efficient and equitable option it is important that a wide range of options is considered. However, there is a need for some filter to be applied as otherwise the list of alternatives would be very large. It is usual to limit the list to the options that are of proven benefit or appear to offer the greatest potential. This emphasizes the link between clinical trials and economic evaluation. In selecting alternatives, it is important that a do-nothing option is considered. In many instances, this is not ethically possible, but where it is possible to include such an option, it provides a valuable benchmark.

Specifying the objective

While the underlying objective may be the achievement of efficiency or equity in the use of resources, conditions that prevail around the investigation may dictate that the measurement of technical efficiency may be the only objective measurable. This will be the case when there are resource constraints about the decision to be made or where treatment is deemed to be essential. The nature of the objectives will also determine the type of analysis to be performed. Where an analysis looks to maximize the efficiency to treatment – technical efficiency – cost minimization and cost effectiveness are appropriate. Where the objective of the analysis is allocative in nature, cost benefit or cost utility is used. If the question seeks to place the decision in terms of a social structure, for instance the total cost to treat a disease against a road programme, cost benefit is the only option.

The objective of the appraisal should also specify the criteria to be adopted with respect to the equity of the programmes. Questions should be asked addressing the variations in health costs and the differences in health that may result from unequitable distributions of services.

Identifying all effects

The epidemiological and clinical evidence of the effects of an intervention need to be linked to the costs and resources consumed as part of this exercise. This process should identify all the beneficiaries of the programme and quantify to what degree they benefit.

There is considerable confusion over what constitutes a cost and what constitutes a benefit – one man's carrot is another's stick – and the debate about costs and benefits is one of the most difficult areas in health economics. New benefits are continually being discovered, which are often outside the conventional ideas of a health benefit. For example, patients may report benefit from ultrasound in pregnancy when there is no clinical benefit to be gained.

Measuring the effects

Measurement of the magnitude of the effects of an intervention is complex. Treatments may produce more than one effect, and the possibility of multiple wanted and unwanted effects has to be considered. The basis of much information of the effect of treatment on the health status of patients is based on clinical trials that often recruit atypical patients and have unidimensional outcomes.

Changes in health status

Changes in health status can be considered in two dimensions: duration of life and quality of life. Changes in the duration of life are relatively easy to quantify as life expectancy under a variety of conditions is measurable. In cost effectiveness analysis, where the outcomes are expressed in terms of a natural unit, for example lives saved, the measurement of quality of life does not feature. However, in cost utility and cost benefit analysis, the quality of life is of prime concern. However, quality of life is a nebulous concept. Quality of life has been defined by a series of domains that reflect the quality of life across the spectrum of human existence. These domains can be related to emotional well being, social functioning, physical status and symptoms and are incorporated into the scales used to measure quality of life. The actual measurement of quality of life takes place by using the scales either in the form of interviews with patients or by the administration of questionnaires. The current measure favoured to measure health status is the quality adjusted life year (QALY).

The measurement of QALYs involves measurements of the changes in health status, together with values attached to these changes. These values are applied not only to the domains of the quality of life, but also to the outcome of the intervention itself. One of the major problems in cost utility analysis is deciding how these values should be obtained, as the assessment of the effectiveness of health care will involve some measurement of improvement in health.

As we have seen, the application of the economic utility to health care is problematical. The inability of the individual to define satisfaction with health care means that QALY measures may be more suitable for studying populations, rather than individuals. This leads to the situation where the results of an evaluation may be unacceptable to the individual but viable on a group basis.

While the measurement of the improvement in health may be feasible, the satisfaction or utility gained from this change relies on an estimation of the preference for that health state over all others. Preferences can be determined in a number of ways, although two methods predominate: standard gamble and time trade-off.

The standard gamble method gives an individual the choice between two outcomes, one offering normal health for a period of time followed by a probability of immediate death, the other offering chronic disease for a period longer than the first option. The probability of death is altered in the first option until the individual feels no preference for either option. This probability is then taken to be the utility of the alternative.

The time trade-off method is simpler as the individual is offered different lengths of time under different states, which are varied until there is no preference expressed. The ratio of the two times is expressed as the preference.

Both of these methodologies require that patients be interviewed about preferences and that those interviewed understand the dynamic nature of the preference. Often, patients without the conditions are asked to express preferences, which is often the major criticism expressed about the derivation of QALYs.

In an attempt to simplify the measurement of utility, other scales have been developed. Time without symptoms or toxicity (TWIST) is one such scale undergoing evaluation. These methods, however, do not resolve the issue surrounding the individual's versus society's viewpoint of treatment. It has been suggested that further divisions are necessary in the case of medical treatments. In life-threatening disorders, the individual's preference may be dominant; however in less serious conditions society's preference should be put first. This suggestion does not solve the problems associated with the measurement of utility associated with medical outcomes. The debate is set to continue.

In addition to the unit problem, the measurement of effects in health economics is also very prone to bias. The bias has three sources. First, economists often rely on second-hand data to assess effectiveness, and the bias contained in these data is often unclear. Second, there is a considerable number of sampling errors to which data collection is especially prone.

- *Selective patient withdrawal.* Here patients are selectively withdrawn from the trial during its length as side-effects and treatment effects become manifest.
- *Skewed costs.* A dead patient uses fewer hospital services than does a live one. Therefore if the treatment is successful, the costs may be skewed against the drug, purely because of increased duration of stay.

The final area concerns missing data. In large complex trials, it is not uncommon for a significant number of variables to be missing. These tend to occur in the least severely ill patients, and therefore the results when analysed are biased.

Valuing the costs and benefits

As we have already stated cost effectiveness analysis and cost utility analysis do not measure benefits in monetary terms. However, the consideration of the costs used in these methods is not easy and great care must be taken.

The costs of treatment are generally considered to be of three types: direct, indirect and intangible. Direct costs are those associated with the treatment, for example drug costs. Indirect costs are treatment related but fall outside the costs associated with the health services; patients travelling to the hospital is a good example. Intangible costs include the costs of suffering and are the most difficult to estimate. For costs to be meaningful, they should ideally be related to the cost of production. The easiest way to achieve this is to make costs marginal, i.e. reflecting the cost of one extra unit of production. This is not always achievable as the production function of health care is so poorly understood. Instead, it is more common to use average costs, where the total costs are divided by the number of units produced. This can cause problems, in particular where benefits may be valued marginally, and we are therefore not comparing like with like.

Ideally, the costs estimated should reflect the economic cost, i.e. the cost should reflect the value in terms of the alternative use to which the resources could be put. This is termed the *opportunity cost*. However, this is in practice most difficult, and pragmatically the market costs are most frequently used, unless it is felt that the market values do not reflect the true cost of an item. This is most likely to arise when there is government subsidy. One of the difficulties with this approach is that the service to be costed is in many cases not part of a market. Here alternative approaches must be used.

The major area in which non-market items have an influence is in the pricing of patient and carer time. One approach is to use an estimation of the value of working time, this leads to the criticism that no individual works for ever and some allowance needs to be made for leisure time. The usual method for handling this dilemma is to perform a sensitivity analysis on the value of leisure time.

A second problem in the analysis of costs is the treatment of capital costs. Capital costs are the costs of purchasing major assets of the programme. These assets are things that have a value outside the programme, including land buildings and equipment. Capital costs differ from other costs in that they represent a major outlay at a single point in time. The value of capital costs also varies with time as the buildings or machines wear out. This is termed depreciation – we are all too familiar with this in terms of cars! Capital costs therefore have two components: the opportunity cost of the initial outlay and the depreciation costs of the asset over time. It is generally accepted that the best way to handle capital costs is to consider them as interest payments on a loan and calculate an equivalent annual cost, much as one would do on a mortgage.

Related to this discussion is the management of overhead costs. The term overhead relates to resources that serve many different departments. Examples include laundry, medical records and portering services. If an individual programme is costed, shares of these items need to be added to the cost of the programme. There is, however, no right way to apportion such costs. Typically, they are apportioned on the basis of utilization of areas and services. This approach involves the costing of all procedures and then adding a portion of overhead costs, depending on the floor space and services used by the procedures. This makes this method time-consuming and difficult. An alternative is the *per diem* approach, in which all the costs associated with a treatment are removed, leaving the hotel costs. The overhead costs are then allocated on the basis of the hotel costs. The disadvantage of this approach is that it assumes that each patient is average in the use of hotel services. Whatever the method used, it is important that it is made explicit in the work considered.

In cost benefit analysis the process is taken one stage further and both costs and benefits are measured in monetary terms. This poses particular problems in health care where many of the benefits are difficult to express in monetary terms as they are not traded. This is particularly relevant to the value of human life.

Human life is often valued by looking at the salaries of workers in high risk industries or by closely examining governmental policy, looking for statements that put a value on life. The problem with both of these methods is that they represent a self-selected group of individuals whose risk may not be borne equally by the rest of society. The valuation of benefits is made more difficult by the inclusion of multiple benefits, for instance the value of a life saved and the benefit to society. In an attempt to include the situation of multiple benefit and improve on the problems of valuing benefits, a number of alternative methods have been described. The predominant methods used are shadow prices and willingness to pay.

Shadow prices

Shadow prices are prices for non-traded commodities that are fixed by the government or the controlling authority. It is argued that such price fixing is legitimate when taxation-based expenditure is involved. The shadow price is set to reflect the consumption of resources by the community, but it is possible to have different prices for the same treatment depending on who is being treated.

It is argued that the use of shadow prices makes decision making explicit, particularly when health is valued as a result of screening exercises. In some aspects, QALY league tables resemble shadow prices, as they reflect the value given to a judgement about the value of a health intervention. The unease about the use of QALY league tables partially stems from their association with shadow prices. It is argued that, as the prices expressed are a community or society valuation, they cannot be applied to individuals. Individuals display a wide range of variation in their valuations, owing to different social and professional interests, so it is argued that QALYs are of little value.

Willingness to pay

Willingness to pay reflects the amount that an individual is willing to pay to receive the benefits of a particular programme or by the level of competition they desire if harm is caused. This ideal is difficult to quantify where social values and benefits are concerned, and the result of exercises are often amalgamated into social benefits. Willingness to pay is often criticized as reflecting the ability of the individual to pay for benefits, i.e. it depends upon an individual's income and wealth. This is particularly a problem when the egalitarian aspects of welfare are considered. It is argued that if willingness to pay reflects the individual's initial endowment, how can willingness to pay result in a fair allocation of resources? This is a deciding feature in health care and it is one of the reasons why willingness to pay has not often been used as a criterion.

The methods used to value the effects of interventions vary widely with the nature of the intervention being studied. In studies involving mainly drug-related effects, the cost of the drugs, the cost of failure of medication and the costs of side-effects are considered to be the most crucial.

Where the items and measurements to be valued are more socially related, there are other difficulties to be faced. For household costs, related market values can be applied. Examples of this can be found where cleaning and hotel services in the home are priced at market values. This is a common practice, but in addition to these costs, it should be remembered that the lost labour and opportunity costs of the relatives should be taken into account. An example of this is in home renal dialysis, where in addition to calculating the costs of the home dialysis, the family and loss, or in some cases gain, in productivity need to be taken into account.

In the final analysis, what really counts is not how effects are valued, but whether they are valued, including an explicit statement of how this was done.

Discounting – the effects of time on the value of costs and benefits

Discounting is one of the most difficult areas of economic evaluation. Its use is based on the idea that individuals would express a preference for the time at which they receive benefits and pay out costs. The reasons for this time preference are complex. They reflect a certain myopia on behalf of individuals who fail to see the long-term benefits of changes and value things more now than in the future. The effect is also due to the increasing age of the individual, better health in older age being valued more highly. The effects of these changes are reflected in the interest rates posted by companies and the government.

Discounting can be applied to both costs and benefits. There is an acceptance that discounts should be applied to costs, but the situation with benefits is less clear. It has been suggested that benefits should be left undiscounted. This poses a risk, however, that the benefits of a project could be improved by postponing it and keeping the costs discounted.

In practice, it is not the practice of discounting that causes problems, but what rate is to be used. The selection of this rate is difficult and two methods may be used to reflect it. First is the real rate, i.e. the interest rate applied at the time of the evaluation. This can be applied but it is difficult to see how a business based rate can be applied to a welfare problem. The second method is based on society's values and in particular society's willingness to forego current benefit for future benefit. In general it is best to include a range of values and try these in the cost benefit calculation. As a guideline the range of values adopted should be consistent with economic values (usually in the range of 2–10%) and:

- include the government interest rate
- include the discount rate used in other studies
- be consistent with current practice; for example, the rate of return on NHS trusts is 6%.

It is important to realize that the discount rate has nothing to do with the rate of inflation. Inflation is accounted for in the valuation by relating all values to the base year.

Assessing risk and uncertainty

As stated in Chapter 1, every economic decision has a degree of uncertainty about it. This uncertainty arises from the assumptions made in the model and also from the actions of the individuals concerned. It is therefore important that uncertainty is taken into account.

The usual method used to account for uncertainty is *sensitivity analysis*. This is a method by which the input parameters are changed to account for the range of values that arise as a result of the uncertainty. While this method accounts for uncertainty, it will not account for missing knowledge.

Related to uncertainty is *risk*. Risk is best considered as the probability that a certain procedure will produce benefit. This is a poorly accommodated area in economic analysis but is nonetheless an important one. The decision to treat a patient, or otherwise, depends very much on the doctor's assessment of the risk. As yet no successful way of incorporating risk has been found.

Assessing equity

After the discussion in Chapter 4, it is important to assess the winners and losers from the changes proposed and whether these changes seem fair. As stated earlier, this is difficult, given the range of projects that may be concerned.

Making recommendations: how is social analysis being used?

The ultimate aim of cost benefit analysis is to inform choice and to influence resource allocation. The current climate of competition in health care offers great opportunity for health economics to make an impact, but progress to date has been slow. The lack of impact may be in part due to the small range of treatments currently being analysed, but there are more fundamental problems.

The first problem lies in the way in which information is presented. It is traditional to impart information by means of a ranking, based on marginal costs and benefits. Many experimenters present the information in the form of a cost per QALY table. This is a ranking of alternatives in the ratio of cost to utility measures, i.e. £ per QALY gained. Some economists have maintained that a cost per QALY ranking offers a prioritization of resources and that those at the top of the list should be invested in before those at the bottom. This approach has been widely criticized. These criticisms feature not only the narrow definition of benefit offered by QALYs, and the use of utility analysis in health care as was mentioned above, but also a more fundamental resistance to the use of ranking methods in health care.

There has been little attention paid to the expression of economic evaluation beyond the QALY league table approach, with the result that there are many interventions that have been shown not to be cost-effective but are still being performed, for example the insertion of grommets. On the opposite side, there are many interventions that are proven to be cost effective that are not being adopted, surfactant use in premature babies being a good example.

At this point it should be emphasized that economic evaluations are only an aid to decision making. When decisions are made, value judgements play a major role and the decision maker may feel that his experience outweighs the assumptions made by the economist. This does not reduce the value of economic analysis – indeed, it helps to explain the decisions that have been made – but economists and study sponsors should bear this in mind when designing studies.

Conclusion

This chapter has introduced the basic processes and concepts involved in cost benefit analysis. It serves as an introduction not only to the methodology but also to the potential pitfalls that can occur.

Further reading

Drummond MF, Soddart GL and Torrance GW (1992) *Methods for the evaluation of health care programmes*. Oxford Medical Publications, Oxford.

6 Dynamic choice and the analysis of uncertainty

Key points from the previous chapter

The use of cost benefit analysis is limited by the economic features of health care; the determination of cost and valuing outcomes is very difficult for the health economist. Partially because of these problems, many of the analyses being performed are cost minimalization in nature. Other features that have an influence include the need to discount the costs and benefits of health care for time and the need to look at the equity of health care benefits.

So far we have been looking at health economic analysis as revealing an all-or-none event. However, this is rarely the case and there is often uncertainty about the results from an analysis. One method for dealing with this uncertainty has already been mentioned in Chapter 5; sensitivity analysis provides a way in which factors with uncertainty in analysis can be checked for their validity. By judicious use of sensitivity analysis much of the variability in analysis can be measured. The use of decision trees and other modelling methods borrowed from operations research enables other uncertainties to be examined. In particular, decision trees are used to look at the uncertainty in extrapolating from populations of trial subjects to individual patients, and in examining the uncertainty associated with time. Therefore the use of decision trees enables economists to take population-based data and model them for individual impact, in both a static and a dynamic manner.

Decision trees

The basic concepts of decision trees were introduced in Chapter 1. By using decision trees the economist is trying to construct a model of the treatment or diagnostic pathway that a patient will follow. The detail of the model will depend on the nature of the analysis. However, it is normal to include the projected outcome of treatment and associated costs.

The outcomes included in decision trees may not be financial in nature. It is possible to include utility measures, such as QALY or natural units. However, it is more normal to use financial outcomes, as the technique was originally designed to do this. In putting outcomes into trees, it is important to remember that discounting will have to be applied to benefits occurring out of the current time period.

Once the tree has been designed and the outcomes determined the model needs populating. In order to complete this the economist must supply two variables. The first is the details of the costs and valuations of the benefits for all the options in the tree. Methods for obtaining these have been mentioned in Chapter 5. The second requirement is for estimates of the probability of the treatment having some effect. This latter variable is very important and is often the major cause of problems in decision analysis.

Estimate of probability

Estimates of the probability for the effectiveness of procedures can be obtained from a variety of sources, the most reliable being randomized controlled clinical trials. However, many trials only contain relatively small numbers. In order to make the analysis meaningful, it is occasionally necessary to combine the results of many different trials. The standard method for doing this is termed meta-analysis, the practice of which is controversial. Trials often differ minutely in their protocol, but these differences can have a major impact on the types of patient recruited. In general meta-analysis is best left to the experts as the technique involves the description of detailed literature search protocols that specify the key words to be used and the inclusion/exclusion criteria for trials to be included. The completion of a meta-analysis also involves detailed statistical tests to ensure that the data collected are homogeneous in content.

An alternative to meta-analysis is the Delphi method. The Delphi technique involves assembling panels of experts on a disease who consider and develop treatment pathways for the disease under consideration. As part of this exercise outcome data from multiple trials can be considered and introduced. Although the Delphi method can be very subjective, it is also very powerful as, if carefully controlled, the results provide simulations of treatments that resemble real life. Delphi techniques can be used to design decision trees, in addition to providing the information about treatment.

In assigning probabilities for the outcomes of treatment, the handling of diagnostic tests deserves special mention. In considering diagnostic tests, there is the chance that tests have both a false negative and false positive outcome. Therefore the probability of a successful outcome will have to be adjusted to reflect these changes. The way this is normally handled is by applying Bayes theorem. A reference for a detailed discussion of Bayes theorem is contained in Further reading below, but when applying the method to diagnostic tests, it has to be borne in mind that the probability, rather than the value of the outcome, is being adjusted downwards.

The provision of cost information is also a vexed question in decision trees. We have already covered the cost problems associated with cost benefit analysis but in handling uncertain decisions cost information is even more important. Arms of the tree will often include treatment patterns that are uncosted. These can either be estimated, bearing in mind the serious deficiencies to estimation as we discussed previously, or can be accurately measured. By constructing a tree the important costs can often be identified and effort put in to obtain these costs.

Dynamic choice and decision trees

It would be possible to construct a series of interlinked decision trees to model the sequential decisions and choices during the management of a patient. However, the resulting analysis would become very complex, especially if a life-long illness were being modelled. Instead of using repeated decision trees it is more common to model the changes in disease by Markov models. These have been widely used in modelling the effects of treatment in mental illness and cardiovascular disease. The idea behind Markov models is that patients can be in a finite set of health status types at any one time. As the disease progresses, they move through the various health states, both forwards and backwards, culminating in death. The rate of transition from state to state is determined by transition probabilities, which are influenced by treatments. As an example, consider a genetic disease that places 10% of its sufferers into long-term care. Therefore the probability of requiring care in any one year is 0.1. In year zero, 10 000 patients are independent, but by the end of the first year this will have reduced to 9000 and by the end of year two to 8100. If a drug reduced the probability to 0.05, i.e. 5%, 500 care episodes would be saved by the end of the first year, as only 500 patients would need care. In this manner the long-term costs are easily calculable. These so-called simple Markov models are useful if the treatment does not vary with the age of the patient, i.e. if a 20-year-old has the same response to treatment as a 60-year-old. Where there is an appreciable change in the effects of treatment with age, it is important then that the analysis should reflect a time-dependent Markov process or Markov chain. Here a whole series of transition probabilities are generated, one for each age band. These chains are repeatably modelled and then averaged to produce a population-based set of transition probabilities that can be used to model costs. Time-dependent Markov processes require a large amount of computer power to operate effectively.

An alternative to Markov processes is the use of simulation. The use of simulation allows the modelling of a wider range of assumptions. Monte Carlo simulations allow the flow of patients to be modelled by applying random events to the stock of health and using treatments to gamble return to health. In this manner, models may be built that permit the insults to be cumulative, rather than constant, and are managed long term. For a detailed discussion of these methods, see the Further reading suggestion.

Choosing the method

Like many tools, models and decision trees are dangerous if used by the inexperienced. The choice of model is best left to the expert, but the simplest model should be used. For example, if treatments do not vary with age, a Markov model is best, and attempts to apply a Markov chain should be resisted.

Conclusion

This chapter has been a very brief discussion into modelling. What is important is not the models themselves but being able to recognize when and where they have been applied. This section ends our discussion of analytical methods on a high note. Models are really just being introduced into health economics and the major growth will be seen in this area.

Further reading

Keeler E (1995) Decision trees and Markov models. In Sloan FA (ed.) *Valuing healthcare*, pp. 185–204. Cambridge University Press, Cambridge.

7 From health economics to information

> **Key points from the previous chapters**
>
> *The various types of health economic models have now been introduced and the advantages and disadvantages are identified. However, one step remains: the turning of health economic models into information that can be used to drive the priority setting and resource allocation processes that are required as part of developing health care markets.*

As we have stressed throughout this text health economics is not about making decisions but about informing choice. As we have already stated markets in health care tend to fail leaving those most in need of care without any. The aim of health economics, therefore is to inform resource allocation. How successful is it?

How are resources allocated?

We have already covered the range of options available for decision makers to allocate resource. To recap, these include market-based, technocratic and democratic methods. In practice, these methods do not act alone but are part of a continuum. The degree of influence each method has depends on factors within the decision.

- *Cost sharing.* Where costs are being shared between a purchaser and a provider, the emphasis is on gaining the best value for money, and market mechanisms will predominate.
- *Behavioural incentives.* These can be likened to cost sharing on an individual basis.
- *Competition among plans.* Where there are more than one set of demands, factors other than value for money come most strongly into play.
- *Education.* Education reduces uncertainty about decisions.

Given these factors the influence of health economic information will vary with the situation and it is hardly surprising that there have been situations in which, despite the existence of valid health economic information, decisions have gone against it.

Where has health economics been used?

The most publicized use of health economics has been in the Oregon Medicaid programme in the USA. Here an attempt was made to define a package of benefits for the Medicaid programme based on the basis of health economic information. The plan was not accepted as there was at federal level competition between health and disability policy. In the final analysis disability was judged to be more important.

Allied to the use of economics in Oregon have been the Australian pharmaceutical guidelines. Decisions to license pharmaceutical drugs in Australia are being made on the basis of the direct costs of the drug. This is justified by saying that illness does not lead to long-term lost production, owing to sickness benefits and unemployment. The use of the Australian guidelines is controversial, but many countries look on in interest.

The Australian and Oregon programmes are the closest that health economics has come to influencing decisions, and even in these programmes several of the conventions mentioned in this book were not used. In particular, not all costs and benefits were considered, long-term effects were omitted and no discounting was applied.

Closer to home, health authorities in the UK are, with mixed success, attempting to apply health economics to purchasing decisions. All too often, the information available on individual decisions is strong enough to inform; however, when taken collectively not enough interventions have information to enable its use. Even where economic information exists, the multiplicity of agendas means that other factors take precedence. For a detailed discussion on this subject, see Further reading below.

What is the problem?

The question is not how to make decisions on economics but how to make the economics fit the decisions. In order to achieve this a careful review of current research is needed. First, studies should no longer be constructed 'willy-nilly' but be based on sound reasoning. Second, outcomes should be quantified in monetary terms wherever possible; economics is a financially based discipline, and its results are most robust when dealing with financial outcomes. Finally, more effort should be put into determining costs and discount rates.

Over the past decade, economics has become a panacea for all ills; it will manufacture drugs better, increase sales and make services more efficient. If economics is to provide useful answers, it should be placed in its proper place and treated like any other clinical activity, conducted in an ethical and scientific manner.

Further reading

Honigsbaum F, Richards J and Lockett T (1995) *Priority setting in action: purchasing dilemmas*. Radcliffe Medical Press, Oxford.

Index